THE VALLEY

Sundress Publications • Knoxville, TN

Library of Congress Control Number: 2021931909
Published by Sundress Publications
www.sundresspublications.com

Editor: Tierney Bailey
Editorial Assistant: Kanika Lawton
Editorial Interns: Nikki Lyssy, Abigail Renner, Claire Shang
Colophon: Text set in Sitka, titles set in Bebas Neue
Cover Design: Kristen Ton
Cover Art: "Weslaco" by Maria and Iris Pérez
Book Design: Tierney Bailey

THE VALLEY

Esteban Rodríguez

ACKNOWLEDGMENTS

Many thanks to the editors of the following magazines and journals in which some of these poems first appeared:

    Bear Review: "East Juárez High" and "Falfurrias"
    Boulevard: "Weslaco"
    Bridge Eight: "Recuerdo: Bare" and "Recuerdo: La migra"
    Gordon Square Review: "Recuerdo: Mexico, 1997"
    Non.Plus Lit: "El río"
    Sundog Lit: "Harlingen," "Progreso," and "Nuevo Progreso"
    The Esthetic Apostle: "SPI"
    Tishman Review: "Recuerdo: Heal"
    UCity Review: "Edcouch," "Elsa," "Queen City," and "San Juan"

A small number of poems first appeared in the chapbook *El Valle* (2019), published by A3 Press. Thank you to Shaun Levin for believing in my work.

Special thank you to my mother and sister, Maria and Iris Pérez, for the photographs included in this collection.

CONTENTS

"The U.S-Mexican border *es una herida abierta* where the Third World grates against the first and bleeds. And before a scab forms it hemorrhages again, the lifeblood of two worlds merging to form a third country—a border culture."
- Gloria Anzaldúa, *Borderlands/La Frontera: The New Mestiza*

WESLACO

Here too the house the boy
      the father bent beneath
the hood of a truck the mother inside
      dusting sweeping adjusting
angel and rooster figurines Here too
      the television novelas the windows
with their blue dusks the sky smuggling
      stars from somewhere up north
or from somewhere down south or from
      any direction that renders them
less than native local less than synonymous
      with the street corner where one pack
of dogs barks at another pack of dogs
      ready to rip flesh apart And here too
the night stale swollen a backdrop
      for barbecues music chitchat
and laughter for rants that become arguments
      for arguments that become threats
for threats that revert back to chitchat
      and laughter and that soften the moment
you come in And whether you enter the scene
      as boy father mother a breeze brushes
a language on your skin one you translate
      the best you can claim as a soul
that's left one body for the next

MERCEDES

Dispute the name not the settlements
       the boom not the claims to a camp
for the war to end all wars not the age of crops
       grapefruit not the families moving in
and out in and out in and out until growth plateaus
       and no one can remember the past
or can see past the Stock Show every year the way
       the trucks and trailers amble in unload
spread their tents set up the Tilt-A-Whirls Himalayas
       the Drop Towers and mini roller coasters
and coasters that from a distance and at dusk
       look like the skeleton of an ancient creature
one you make your way toward knowing that as you
       come nearer nearer you'll lose the illusion
forget what narrative you were inventing and replace it
       with description: metal rust untrustworthy wood
a line that grows longer by the minute a crowd
       that forms and the image of you looking
at yourself in the center doused in laughter and ready
       as the deep-fried darkness thickens
to slip away pretend you were never here

EAST JUÁREZ HIGH

And still the words don't come don't cross
        the borders of your mouth don't sound
how your maestra says they should sound
        too low too soft too white to claim
these strange conjugations as your own even though
        you know that if born half a century ago
you'd have been raised with the right pitch and tone
        that you wouldn't as you do now feel
you're someone else an imposter pretender a student
        who despite attempts to memorize phrases
like a script can't speak enough Spanish just like
        his mother couldn't speak enough English
couldn't answer the questions from Ms Smith
        And even when your mother responded gave
the right date name a hard concept and explanation the accent
        was too harsh Mexican too foreign to sound
correct and she was scoffed at berated sent to the office
        belittled enough to confess this to you and for you
to invent her punishment believe that after sitting
        through the principal's lecture she was told to bear
her tongue lips and with a pen was shown the ways
        language can be carved on flesh

PROGRESO

And with no insurance no savings
      than what remained from my father's
paychecks she'd return to her home country
      take me with her explain the longer
you neglect something the more it becomes useless
      And though I was unsure why she described
her teeth like this or why when we arrived
      at the dentist the lobby smelled
like cotton candy I remember Progreso the city
      before Mexico the way it rose into view
like a lost civilization buildings graffitied weathered
      cars parked on the side of the road sunburnt
and abandoned And there were the stands before
      the bridge the one that sold pottery
the one that sold piñatas the one that your mother
      would stop at study the maze of random
objects the car parts jewelry the necklaces
      you wanted to touch thinking the shells
were really bones and that the woman who owned
      the stand had found them buried in this stretch
of earth wanted to show if just to herself that the dead
      could be resurrected that things
could go on living if we believed they could

RECUERDO: SUMMER, 1996

Like a stray   the wind unfurls on mounds
of threadbare tires   rows of plantless pots

rusted rims and hubcaps   stacked cinder blocks
where a doorless car   whose model and year

have long been corroded   made anonymous
by the sun   sits on top of them like a post-

apocalyptic prop   You survey the clutter
question if the scene is indeed what you once

heard a boy call the Rapture   or something
akin to the feeling that when you gaze at

the surrounding acres of half-dead or dying
crops   how they foreground the houses

that have become foreclosed silhouettes
this semblance of a neighborhood has been

forgotten   and the world has moved on
framing the horizon with heavy-handed themes

of loneliness and loss   The wind yawns
slumps against the yard's chain-link fence

where mange-infested mutts sneak beneath
like nomads completing their exodus

And you study the blue plastic pool propped
against it   its inside warped and dented

filled with dead gnats   legless insects
and those dimples your mother hammers out

with her fists and elbows   evening
their rough and pointed edges   She flips

the pool over   and with the same obligation
with which your father throws Hefty bags

of monthly trash into a pile   douses
diesel and sets it on fire   she tosses it

in the middle of the yard   and with a hose
she handles like a bullwhip   rinses

the gunk   fills water to the top   But oh
how grime rises   clumps   leeches

to your skin as you move through the murkiness
splash around   pretend you're a shark

or the Loch Ness monster   or anything
that camouflages you so well with the water

that you come out hours later as a pruned
figure lurking onto the lawn   shaking

the water off   and adjusting to the way
the bruised rays of sunlight make you feel

all gooseflesh and new

RECUERDO: HEAL

Before my mother conceded my body
to a clinic   to cotton swabs   stethoscopes

tongue depressors   injections   suppositories
generic prescriptions   and lollipops I'd leave with

without the strength to lift them   I'd be subjected
to rounds of Robitussin   expired Nyquil

cocktail after cocktail of nondescript medicines
from Mexico   of those bronze and maroon

liquids she insisted were both natural and sweet
and that   regardless of their consistency

would keep my fever from rising   forming
into bronchitis   pneumonia   ancient strains

of influenza   tuberculosis   or whatever illness
made my breathing sound like an imitation

of my grandfather's   and led her to knead clumps
of VapoRub across my chest all evening

In the morning   when the coughing returned
and the temperature my mother gaged

with her hand still felt warm   I'd toss back
another dose of something I couldn't pronounce

along with bottles of Sprite   7-Up   salt water
I'd guzzle down   knowing the remedies

would turn into dollar store candles of saints
on the stove   into the cleaning of the house

with incense   or into me lying half-naked
on the couch   watching my grandmother crack

the cold egg she'd pass over my body
into a bowl   and waiting   as she'd pray

in languages I never heard   for the yolk
to curdle   for the symptoms to no longer

claim me as their source

RECUERDO: NUKED

When our pantry was empty
and the meat that sat defrosting

for weeks had turned to mush
my mother searched the back of our fridge

till she exhumed stacks of Tupperware
and placed   like a priest stocking

the tabernacle with wine   bread
what she could mix into a miracle of a meal

inside the microwave   Overworked
my favorite appliance droned   gave me up

the nights I   half-asleep and starved   heated
Hot Pockets   pizza   or whatever I could find

that had the right amount of cheese on it
and that melted   bubbled and oozed

onto a turntable speckled with chicken noodle soup
we ate at the end of every month   how the bowls

were always too hot   and how   when I
became in charge of taking our dinner out

my mother sidelined with cracked
and ulcer-ridden feet   I stood farther away

from the microwave   concerned   if indeed
what the boys at school said was true

that the closer I was   waiting for our food
the more the rays would cause the most important

part of me to either shrink or disappear

RECUERDO: FOIL

Not just for leftovers
tortillas   lidless jars and bowls

but for my father's science
the technician in him that ripped

sheets of foil   wrapped
the scrunched pieces on the TV's

antennas   convinced the image
wouldn't freeze   stammer   slow

wouldn't ruin the favorite parts
of his shows   would   if squeezed

and twisted just right   calm
the storm of static   just as rolls

of it would keep   during God's
spiteful summers   every window

in our house cool   turn our living room
into a small dark arctic

or into a space where my father
could doze   and where I

out of boredom   could take
the leftover foil   mold it

into ray guns   sabers   or into hats
I'd place on my head and his

ready to shield our secrets
from the world

NUEVO PROGRESO

No bridge this time No sun singeing its spite
       on our faces necks No walking like fugitives
watching the seated and serape-wrapped women beg
       or saying no to the boys selling candy chiclets
or ignoring as best we can the old legless men in wheelchairs
       shaking their cups on the corner mumbling
what I think are prayers but are probably visions
       prophesies of what this earth will soon become
if it can become something more than the hum and honks
       of idle cars than vendors outside their shops shouting
like they have secrets to auction off No this time we sit
       in the van drive from the bridge into town
pretend the AC works pretend that we're here because
       we have a choice that my mother has insurance
doesn't need to see a doctor that the bed rest Sprite
       and prayers worked and that the expired pills
she took as a last resort made the coughing go away
       Yes this is just assurance a trip to put her mind
at ease and to remind herself no matter how much
       it isn't true that because she no longer lives here
she can manage how her body heals

DONNA

In the city with a heart in the heart of the Valley
        you smudge the haze off the edges of a scene
see vans trailers see the way a tent unfolds
        like a moth see the signs staked crookedly
across the lot advertising to the highway and the world
        beyond a circus a three-night extravaganza
filled with elephants lions with trapeze artists who will bend
        the laws of gravity leave us feeling like we've never
felt before or so the signs imply and because you
        in this moment are a child once again you beg
your mom to take you claim that this week you'll be good
        that you won't ask for candies toys won't refuse
to do your chores and when at the show you'll stay as still
        as possible will watch as the elephants play dead
as the acrobats swing from bar to bar as the clowns trip over
        one another and their wigs fall off reveal a balding
head you refuse to let distract you from the truth you believe in:
        all of this real and one day you too will shed
your ordinariness be someone else

MCALLEN

In Little México she says *Tienen dresses ahí*
          And after my cousin smiles nods and says
thank you to my mother she looks at me asks if I want
          to shop for my quince too which I laugh at
and she laughs at and I laugh at more until we arrive
          in Little México and after shopping at store
after store after store I begin to feel that I do
          that months from now when I turn fifteen
I'll want the gown the ball room the gathering of family
          and friends the dance with my father
so he can acknowledge even if the quince says I am
          that although I'm not yet a man I will be soon
and like my cousin who at the end of the night
          will feel like someone else I'll feel brand new
or new enough to not think about the daughter my mother
          never had or that at celebrations like these
I'm sitting in the back wondering if when my time comes
          I'll have my cake and eat it too

FALFURRIAS

Though he's practiced it the *Yes* the *Sir*
       the *American citizen* he pauses lets
his accent slip lets his forehead sweat lets
       a small smile form on the corner of his lips
as if it alone could disarm suspicion as if the agent
       just as brown as him would no longer see
the otherness in his skin and he'd be waved through
       wished the best not thought about again
But no My father's told to pull over step out go into
       an office while I whose English is shy but fluent
must sit outside on a bench guess what they're asking him
       if they suspect he forged his documents
if they think he's not who he says he is And I know he
       no longer is when he comes out tells me
without a word to get into the car and drives us off
       half embarrassed half relieved and sure
that when he crosses the checkpoint again he'll be
       whoever they expect him to be

EL RÍO

Like a newborn   he emerges   crawls onto the riverbank   Because the moon deems itself
holy   it christens him   offers a glow night   ordained with its own agenda   erases from his
skin   peeling off the afterbirth of mud   water   of starlight that leeched onto his shoulders
neck   In the distance   searchlights scythe the darkness   Coyotes eat their young   And as
he crawls farther up   hieroglyphs the earth with knees   nails   palms   you don't see him
as your father   don't see him as the man whose silence shaped you growing up   No   To-
night he is just a figure   a shadow joining other shadows that have crossed the river   and
that   like your notion of a body pardoned of its soul   wanders across the land   searches for
whatever brings him closer to atonement   closure

Nightfall   And your father finds himself in a factory again   skulking   as the last of the river molts from his skin   to the middle of the floor   where a row of headless scarecrows hangs on meat hooks   sways like slaughtered pigs   or like heretics made into examples displayed for the sinful   the sinless   He reaches up   touches what's left of their legs   and when the aisle ends   he nears a table filled with doll heads   each blindfolded   each a symbol he fails to understand   wondering if the gashes double as hieroglyphs   or if there's a reason why some have their jaws crushed   caved in   hair matted   wires sprouting from the bottoms of their necks   programmed with a voice that recites a sermon when he turns the switch   and that he hears   between the calls for repentance   cry his name   urge him to remove his clothes   and to lie sprawled on the table   wait   as the babble continues   for darkness to place coins on his eyes   lips

In this version   the river turns to concrete   and your father stops flailing   controls his arms again   rises to his feet   Like a creature about to enter extinction   he walks this once-river   until he comes upon a building   gray and windowless   but framed around a door men   just as crosshatched and faceless as him   step into   And for you   son   observer writer absolved of exodus and responsibility   the symbolism is easy   heavy-handed even but stark enough to describe   detail   depict with all your synonyms   and to express into a scene where your father falls to his knees   prays   aware the ground he believes in   will not always remain

In each of us there's a river   and though you want to believe your father when he tells you this   you find nothing when you look   just a riverbed filled with parentheses of jawbones ribs   with mounds of shredded plastic   cardboard   clothes   and   each time you place yourself in the middle of it   with a makeshift coffin   small and made of branches   twigs or in some cases   when the scene cradles dusk on the horizon   with teeth   millions of them   rotted   or fitted with silver caps   or just as plain as the ones you begin pulling from your mouth   and which you hope   if the time should come   your father will find   identify them as his son's

Even in sleep   my father's at the river's edge   gazing   some nights   at the fires spiting darkness on the other side   unsure if they're signals   accidents   or warnings to him   and men like him   that he shouldn't cross   that if he does what awaits once he's trudged miles of corpses and sagebrush   is another river   this one wider   deeper   molded out of adjectives he's never heard of   and which could care less if he jumps in   dog-paddles against the current   and watches as the river extends   swells until he can no longer see the bank   and he must turn back   or stay if his limbs grow numb   accept the water that fills his mouth the nothingness he prays he has the strength to wake up from

River long gone   your father trudges a desert filled with suitcases   baby seats   abandoned sedans and SUVs   until   days later   he stumbles on a cluster of tents   gazes   from behind half-buried wagons and cow carcasses   at the parody of a baroness   barefoot   braless gnawed turkey leg in hand   She tears through its skin   Grease drips from her bearded jaw and as she tosses the bone to a wake of buzzards chained together at the neck   a jester staggers into view   waves his bottle like a wand   and attempts to conjure the presence of his troupe   to explain how in a dream once   cast to a desert flanked by fences and wet pavement   suited figures around him drew a circle in the sand   tossed in their passports wallets   keys and wedding rings   whatever bore enough meaning to leave an impression and to compel the jester to place a hula hoop at their feet   and watch as they stepped into it   ready to give up what they knew they'd never be

All summer it rains   and the river   burdened with garbage   corpses   bears descriptions of
the biblical   a flood your father's been casted to the middle of   thrashing   shouting   cursing
God's version of justice   and realizing   as the sky above him swells   darkens   that this
is punishment   that he'll drown and drift for days until his body washes up   and like any
body sprawled on a bank   he will be found   poked at   spoken to in a language of doubt
and dragged to a place where you   eventually   can view your once-father   promise him to
not suffer such fate

Because no one's looking   a wall is built   and with nowhere else to go   the men who've yet to scale it make the ground it casts its shadow on their home   As you walk amongst them   unsure how you got here   or if any part of this is real   you find a man you believe to be your father   only he doesn't remember you   can't recall how he crawled from the river once   staggered till dawn rendered him reborn   or of the decades he spent on the other side of earth   knowing   as you know now   that if he was caught   tried   expelled   the path leading back would not welcome his return

After the storm   the river relents   and as the names it kept for years rise to the top   you write them down

Sergio Guzmán   Isabella García   Samuel Rodríguez López   Lucas Martínez Edwin Hernández   Gabriela Muñoz Gómez   Natalia Martínez   Victoria Ochoa   Valeria Navarro   Juan Figueroa   Carlos Molina   Guadalupe Aguirre   Emma Fuentes   Antonia Cabrera   Samantha De León   Juan Esteban Santos Hernández   Javier Villarreal   Jesús Calderón   Dylan Camacho   Esteban Salas   Camila Martínez   Diego Serrano   Sebastián Colón Benjamín Rosales   Edwin Rivas   Tomás Morales Molina   Martín Vargas   Fernanda Robles Sara Castro   Vanessa Garza   Fátima Flores Rodríguez   Olivia Mendez   Héctor Pérez   Marcos Grimaldo   Paulina Ríos   Guadalupe Salazar   María Peña   Carolina Rubio   Gael Cavazos Oscar Martínez   Sergio Coronado   Alma Quiroz   Luisa Garza   Patricia Alfaro   María Mejía José Hernández   Juan Hinojosa   Luis Zepeda   Natalie Leyva   Evelyn Benavides   Alexander Uribe   Diego Fuentes Axel Osorio   Jonathan Pérez   Angelina Peralez   Migdalia Yañez   Alexa Nieto   Carla Ybarra   Juan Manuel Serna   Cristian Quiroz   Patricio Rodríguez   Alan Esquivel   Milton Parra   Pedro Sierra   Christian Correa   Paola Reyna   Rocío Quiñones Fabiana Bernal   María Villalobos   Matthew Trejo   Edwin Rocha Flores   Diana Esparza Marcos Córdova   Simón Salgado   Ian Perales Sosa   Anthony Murillo   Alonso Baca   Ana Montes   Violeta Soliz   Arian Lima Nieto   Pilar Palacios   Ángel Samaniego   Fernando Garces Leonardo Garces   Ignacio Riojas   Maximiliano de la Rosa   Eduardo Huerta   Christopher Beltrán   Allison Dávila   Jamie Benitez   Brianna Cuevas   Brayan Quintero   Abigail Guevara Junior Bautista   Juliana Osorio   Andrés Ponce   Ruth Uribe   Naomi Montes   Juana Rodríguez Alexa Robles   Rodrigo Ibarra   Bryan Guerra   Juan Pablo Treviño   Jaime Guerra   Litzy Pacheco   José Barrera   Luz Escobar   Javier Salazar   Andrea Camacho   Luis Cavazos   Norma Perales   Letti Cruz   Juan Bautista   Rebeka Solis   Anayeli López   David Barrios   Lola Benavides   Vanessa Baca Vargas   Valencia Mata   Cristian Mendez Ochoa   Lupe Velez Rigoberto Castañeda   Anibal Rodríguez   Natalia Domínguez   Jason Guerrero   Julian Escobar Ignacio Sosa   Ruby Trejo   Alan Trejo   Briza Figueroa   Edwin Coronado   Arleth Molina Sergio De León   Fernando Fuentes   Eduardo Nuñez   John Ortiz   Miguel Romero   José Luis Díaz   Adriana Ramirez   Teresa Vasquez   Margarita Castro Chavez   Araceli Gómez   Gloria Díaz   Ana María Ramos   Jesús Garza   Ricardo Soto   Gerardo Ortega Ruíz   Arturo Delgado Leticia Peña   Josefina Rubio   Carlos Contreras   Raúl Estrada   Juan Vega   María Luisa Santiago   Isabela Maldonado   Patricia Silva López   Elizabeth Fernandez   Anneth Sandoval Stephanie Padilla   Alyssa Robles   Sara Salinas   Gloria Mejía   Tabitha Lara   Kati Cervantes Vicente Gallegos   Lorena Durán   Alyssa Aguirre   Pablo Colón   Geronimo Rosales   Rodrigo Ayala Santos   Isaac Rivas   Kimberly Villarreal   Lavina Treviño   Alma Cantú   Luciano Meza Emiliano Cisneros   Jonathan Esparza   Marcos Guevara   Mauricio Quintero   Ian Ponce   Dylan

Arroyo   Paloma Villanueva   Gael Duarte   Irene Rojas   Carolina Padilla   Ivana Jiménez
Katia Reyes   Josefa Díaz   Romina Rivera   Paula García   Alexa Rodríguez   Héctor Flores
Vicente Torres   Esteban Gónzalez Mario Morales   Mary Castillo   Antonia Valdez   Miguel
Marquez   Samuel Moreno   Rosa Herrera   Gabriela Ríos   Margarita Cavazos   Yolanda
Mendez   Araceli Bautista   Luisa Leyva   Miranda Uribe   Camilo Quiroz   Ramiro Palacios
Alejandra Baca   Veronica Bernal   Carla Villalobos   Loretta Vasquez   Jorge Escobar   Roberto
Cisneros   Abel Hinojosa   Diego García   Nicolás Ibarra   Kevin Pacheco   Pablo Montes   Aaron
Parra   Oscar Huerta   Elena de la Rosa   Martha Garces   Luna Guerrero   Angelina Samaniego
Violeta Yañez   Bianca Osorio   David Barrera   Ignacio Rodríguez   Lucas Molina Trejo   Alonzo
Serna   Ruby Rojas   Julian Esparza   Alyssa Robles   Rebecca Flores Rodríguez   Gerardo
Delgado   Antonio Meza   Mario Cantú   Abel Hernández   Paulina Velez   Alexis Sandoval
Alexander Villanueva   Marcos Medina   Julieta Herrera   Steven Vargas Guzmán   Yolanda
Ortiz   Sara Castillo   Melissa Castro   Rodrigo Valdez   Lupe Nuñez   Cristopher Vega
Josefina Aguilar   Norma García   Ashley Pérez   Naomi Reyes   Litzy Gutierrez   Benjamín
Torres   Luciano Valdez   Ricardo Ortega   Alonso Estrada   Axel Gallegos   Eduardo de la Cruz
Brianna Mora   Juliana Melendez   Andres Zuniga   Juana Zavala   Julian Ponce   Cristian
Abellano   Evelyn Martínez   Enma Beltran   Juan Salgado   Jamie Rosas   Abigail Dávila   Junior
Vargas   Natalia Esparza   Héctor Mata   Guadalupe Macías   Samantha Pacheco   Oscar Solis
Luis Rocha Figueroa   Sergio Guerrero   Gael Alvarado   Juan Guzmán   Alma Vargas   Matthew
Rodríguez   Bryan Domínguez   Juan Pablo González   Isidro Rivera   Luz Garces   Carla
Olivarez   Diego Lugo   Rafael Espinoza   Leonardo Quintero   Alexa Bravo   Anthony Cabrera
Pedro Fuentes   Milton Molina   Angelina Figueroa   María Luisa Navarro   Sara Ochoa   Alan
Martínez   Mauricio Muñoz   Gloria Gómez   Valencia Hernández   Kevin Martínez   Esteban
López Rodríguez   Rodney García   Emmy Serna   Ana María Reyna   José Molina   Fernando
Trejo   Fátima Rodríguez   Martín Osorio   Sebastián Yañez   Edwin Castillo   Antonia Morales
Olivia González   Lucas Torres   Tomás Flores   José Rivera   Jesús Díaz   Anibal Reyes   Luna
Escobar   Araceli Jiménez   Margarita Padilla   Mary Nuñez   Mario Fuentes   Esteban De León
Vicente Coronado   Héctor Figueroa   Alexa Trejo   Alexis Molina Trejo   Paula Sosa   Romina
Escobar   Josefa Guerrero   Katia Domínguez   Ivan Rodríguez   Carolina Casteñeda   Irene
Velez   Linda Mendez Mata   Teresa Baca Ochoa   Gael Benavides   Paloma Barrios   Dylan
López   Ian Solis   Mauricio Bautista   Marcos Cruz   Jonathan Perales   Emiliana Cavazos
Kimberly Ortiz   Isaac Ortega   Jacobo Maldonado   Rodrigo Correa   Geronimo Salinas   Pablo
Aguirre   Gloria Rojas   Alyssa Garces   Vicente Gallegos   Lorena Durán   Alyssa Aguirre
Pablo Colón   Geronimo Rosales   Rodrigo Ayala Santos   Isaac Rivas   Kimberly Villarreal
Lavina Treviño   Alma Cantú   Luciano Meza   Emiliano Cisneros   Jonathan Esparza   Marcos
Guevara   Mauricio Quintero   Ian Ponce   Dylan Arroyo   Paloma Villanueva   Alonso Baca   Ana

Montes Violeta Soliz Arian Lima Nieto Pilar Palacios Ángel Samaniego Fernando Garces Leonardo Garces Ignacio Riojas Maximiliano de la Rosa Eduardo Huerta Christopher Beltrán Allison Dávila Jamie Benitez Brianna Cuevas Brayan Quintero Abigail Guevara Junior Bautista Juliana Osorio Andrés Ponce Ruth Uribe Naomi Montes Juana Rodríguez Kati Ybarra Tabitha Samaniego Lorena Palacios Sara Nieto Alyssa Solis Stephanie Montes Arleth Baca Elizabetha Murillo Patricia Perales Isabela Sosa María Luisa Salgado Juan Córdova Raúl Esparza Carlos Rocha Josefina Flores Trejo Leticia Villalobos Arturo Bernal Gerardo Quiñones Ricardo Reyna Jesús Correa Ana María Sierra Gloria Parra Araceli Esquivel Margarita Rodríguez Teresa Yañez Adriana Pacheco José Escobar David Barrios Lola Benavides Vanessa Baca Vargas Valencia Mata Cristian Mendez Ochoa Lupe Velez Rigoberto Castañeda Carlos Molina Guadalupe Aguirre Emma Fuentes Antonia Cabrera Samantha De León Juan Esteban Santos Hernández Javier Villarreal Jesús Calderón Dylan Camacho Esteban Salas Camila Martínez Diego Serrano Sebastián Colón Benjamín Rosales Edwin Rivas Tomás Morales Molina Martín Vargas Fernanda Robles Sara Castro Vanessa Garza Fátima Flores Rodríguez Olivia Mendez Héctor Pérez Marcos Grimaldo Paulina Ríos Guadalupe Salazar María Peña Ignacio Mejía Leonardo Aguirre Fernando Cervantes Ángel Lara Pilar Durán Ariana Salinas Violeta Robles Ana Padilla Alonso Sandoval Anthony Fernández Cruz Ian Silvia López Abraham Maldonado Isaac Santiago Simón Vega Marcos Estrada Diana Contreras Edwin Rubio Matthew Peña Paul Delgado María Ortega Fabiana Ruíz Rocío Soto Paola Garza Christian Ramos Pedro Fuentes Milton Díaz Alan Gómez Benjamín Castro Jamie Rosas Abigail Dávila Junior Vargas Natalia Esparza Héctor Mata Guadalupe Macías Samantha Pacheco Oscar Solis Luis Rocha Figueroa Sergio Guerrero Gael Alvarado Juan Guzmán Alma Vargas Matthew Rodríguez Bryan Domínguez Juan Pablo González Isidro Rivera Luz Garces Carla Olivarez Diego Lugo Rafael Espinoza Leonardo Quintero Alexa Bravo Anthony Cabrera Pedro Fuentes Milton Molina Angelina Figueroa María Luisa Navarro Sara Ochoa Alan Martínez Mauricio Muñoz Gloria Gómez Valencia Hernández Kevin Martínez Esteban López Rodríguez Rodney García Emmy Serna Ana María Reyna José Molina Fernando Trejo Fátima Rodríguez Christopher Rodríguez Eduardo Quiroz Maximiliano Serna Allison Ybarra Jamie Nieto Brianna Solis Luz Lima Nieto José Montes Litzy Yañez Kelsey Perales Juan Pablo Paredes Brayan Osorio Rodrigo Fuentes Rigoberto Uribe Alex Benavides Juana Leyva Estefani Zepeda Ruth Hinojosa Juliana Alfaro Carla Sierra Juan Manuel Parra Cristian Rocha Flores Patricio Murillo Alexander Palacios Jean Escobar Natalie Guerra Luisa Ponce Paloma Villanueva Gael Duarte Irene Rojas Carolina Padilla Ivana Jiménez Katia Reyes Josefa Díaz Romina Rivera Paula García Alexa Rodríguez Héctor Flores Vicente Torres Esteban Gónzalez Mario Morales Mary Castillo Antonia

Valdez   Miguel Marquez   Samuel Moreno   Rosa Herrera   Gabriela Ríos   Margarita Cavazos Yolanda Mendez   Araceli Bautista   Luisa Leyva   Miranda Uribe   Camilo Quiroz   Yolanda Ortiz   Sara Castillo   Melissa Castro   Rodrigo Valdez   Lupe Nuñez   Cristopher Vega Josefina Aguilar   Norma García   Ashley Pérez   Naomi Reyes   Litzy Gutierrez   Benjamín Torres   Luciano Valdez   Ricardo Ortega   Alonso Estrada   Axel Gallegos   Eduardo de la Cruz Brianna Mora   Emiliano García   Nicolás Contreras   Lupe Esparza   Ivan Ibarra   Pablo López Ignacio Reyes   Katia Pacheco   Gabriela Ochoa   Sara Rivas   Guadalupe Rubio   Gael Grimaldo Samantha Guzmán   Ashley Hernández   Oscar Benavides   Antonia Molina   Samuel Barrera Alma Serrano   Natalia Bernal   Ángel Flores Rocha   Evelyn Guzmán   José Luis Díaz   Kevi Solis   Anthony Guerra   Venicio Quiroz   Ian Estrada   Paloma Villanueva   Gael Duarte   Irene Rojas   Carolina Padilla   Ivana Jiménez   Katia Reyes   Josefa Díaz   Sergio Guzmán   Isabella García   Samuel Rodríguez López   Lucas Martínez   Edwin Hernández   Gabriela Muñoz Gómez   Natalia Martínez   Victoria Ochoa   Valeria Navarro   Juan Figueroa   Carlos Molina Guadalupe Aguirre

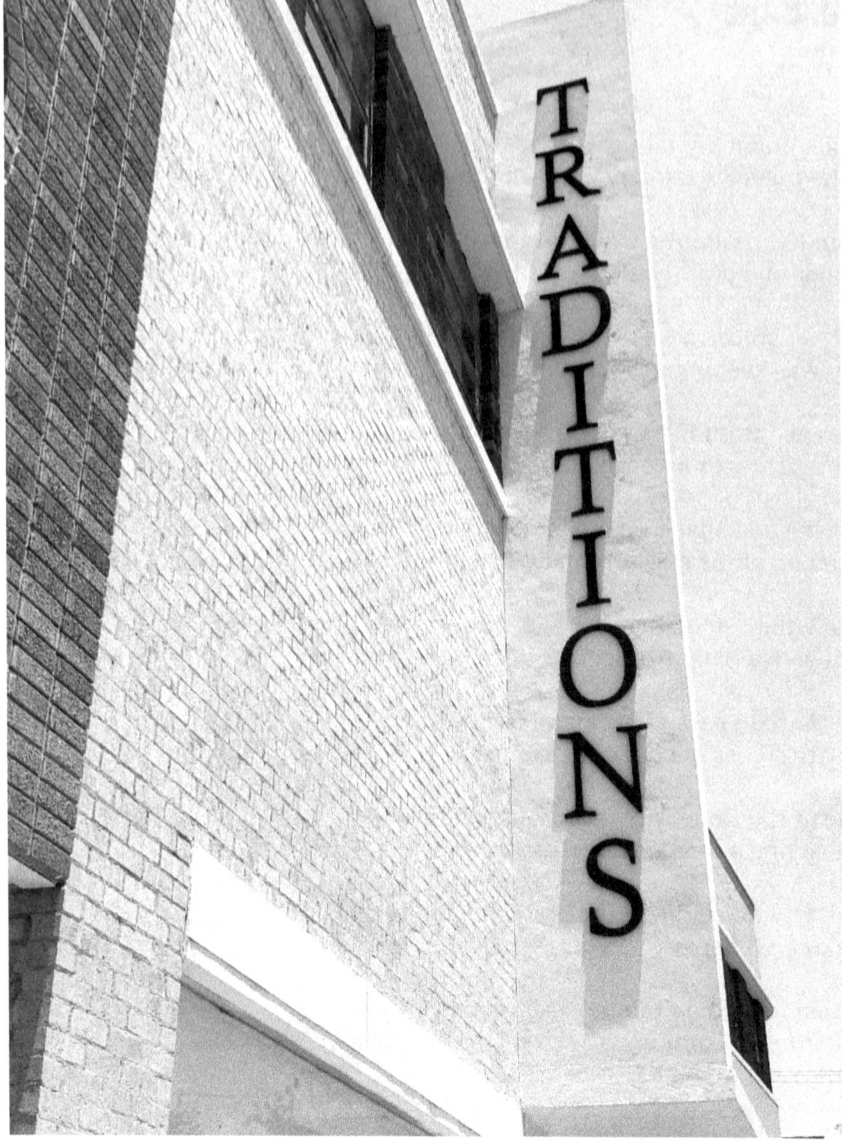
TRADITIONS

RECUERDO: BARE

Once   I walked in on my father undressing
watched as he tugged his underwear and jeans

down his lean light-complexioned thighs
For what either one of us could have mistaken

for eternity   we stood motionless   questioning
what exactly was keeping us locked in this position

if really   we each wanted to see across time
he to study the features he once embodied

me to accept the odd shape I'd one day become
And as I gazed up at his gut   I remembered the linemen

at school   how they stood beneath the showers
in the morning   washing themselves with bars

of soap they shared   passed back and forth
and that they tried   so desperately   to drop

in the middle of the floor   My father lifted his jeans
said without saying a word   that I should shut the door

and when I did   walked down the hall with the image
of a man looking vulnerable   I was thrust back into

the locker room   avoiding the upperclassman who
as they stood around   propped their legs on the bench

were unafraid if their towels slipped   uncovered
that part of themselves that if you saw   you acted

as best you could   like you hadn't at all   which is why
that evening   as we sat for dinner   I kept my eyes

on my plate   and cut the meat my father cooked
with a knife I had no idea how to use

RECUERDO: ELEGY FOR MY MOTHER'S NIGHTGOWN

From a distance   it shined like silk or satin
confident in its purpose   length   in the way

it molded to my mother's body   made no excuses
for her stomach   waist   or for the years when

the flesh behind her arms began to sag   stretching
the sleeves till they unstitched the most delicate

sections of thread   Still   it never gave in
and when the extra pounds disappeared

and every part of her that was once round lost
its shape   she continued to move in it as if

it wouldn't slip   wouldn't bare her breasts
when she kissed my forehead and tucked me in

On nights when I caught a glimpse   lost
momentarily   in that stretch-marked abyss

and the image of my mother buried in that white
frayed and wrinkled fabric played again   again

I pictured her as a mannequin   and placed her
in the mall   where she stood with her hands

on her hips   watching a flow of women
approach the store window   gaze up and wonder

if that black see-through garment she wore
deserved to be felt on their skin

RECUERDO: LOWRIDER

Though the lots were random
abandoned mall   plaza   moonlit fields

beside a gas station   their shows
were filled with music   beer

with men old enough to be my father
And though I   sometimes   found myself

smuggled here   gawking at the trophies
banners   at the top-crop girls moving

from car to car   against my uncle
no one cared   the focus on the murals

of howling wolves   deserts   crosses
of mythic jungles and new universes

splayed on the hoods   trunks   doors
or on the hydraulics wired to make

the cars jump higher   kiss the star-filled
weekend air   or on the countless hours

devoted to each car   a labor my uncle
on the driveway of my grandparents'

house   poured into his Chevy Impala
content   as always   to shine the grille

strip radio wires   or to kneel by the inside
of the driver's seat door   where

after cutting a mirror   he'd arrange
the rectangles into a panel   see

reflections of himself   the one
with sweat running down his temples

the one who was twenty-six   still lived
at home   the one who would one day arrive

at a show with a car of his own   explain
to the crowd how the engine worked

how the rims were 22 inches   custom
chrome   and how the steering wheel

like all things that represent control
looked as though it was made

entirely of gold

RECUERDO: ALMANAC

August ends   And as our fields
begin to look like cemeteries   and the heat

keeps our crops in a state of limbo
I again page through every date   tide

moon and sun in my father's almanac
As archaic as the Yellow Pages delivered

every year   my mother sees his book
as *nada más que mierda*   or   on days

when a pack of wine coolers has coursed
through her throat   she slurs and calls it

a piece of horseshit   then says *I told you so*
and watches   by the kitchen sink   my father

stare at the table   drum his fingers
like thunderstorms   contemplate

the harvest   why June and July fell short
of conditions he invested in   but which he read

into the way one determines their day
around a horoscope   extracting meaning

from low percentages   from proverbs
centered on the movements of cattle

insects   on what time of day the fowls
chose to roost   or on anything in those calendars

that made him feel better about a landscape
that had yet to yield anything in return

How he says all this without saying a word
then rises from the table   leaves the room

ready to sow all of himself
into the scalded earth

ELSA

It began with measurements napkin sketches
           of ideas for a driveway Then began the work
after work the sense that when my father mixed
           and poured cement he had every right to evenness
that after decades of calling this soil home he should
           no longer have to park his truck on unsteady
ground on that foundation where our house was built
           and where before the driveway was close
to being done he'd begin building something else extend
           the porch fix the roof put up the frame
for a kind of garage where he could put his tools
           or where he could rest hang out not have to go
inside the house not have to explain to my mom why
           the driveway was the way it was and how it took time
that he couldn't rush that like anything good he had to let
           his projects sit simmer take on lives of their own
and become months or years down the road a thing
           he could look at the way I imagined God looked at us
perfect despite its flaws

EDCOUCH

He knows you have no interest that cars
        and engines fifteen years and counting
are still not your thing And yet he brings you along
        makes you get off says it's good to get
some sun But here in the yard of your father's friend's
        house you don't care for vitamin D care less
for the work that begins on your father's truck
        or for the way your father turns around
as if you'd have a change of heart be willing to learn
        and lend a hand No here in some colonia
whose name you can't pronounce you care only for
        the packs of dogs those strays that lay on
the surrounding yards or near the potholes on the street
        where the asphalt ash-colored and lumpy
singes their matted and hairless bodies and gives them
        a warmth you try to give when you walk near
kneel and thrust out your hand as if they'd understand
        the emptiness in your palm as if you alone
could make their suffering disappear

SAN JUAN

Like a mushroom cloud smoke billows
       from the hood and you think it's too early
that trucks shouldn't break down in the morning
       that neither you nor your father deserve
this hassle nor this humidity that begins to turn
       your flesh into putty and that prompts you
even before your father opens the hood studies
       the engine to walk away to try to find a reason
behind such luck in the sky horizon in the fields
       where you see what you first think
are scarecrows then realize are workers men picking
       cabbage or a crop you've never heard of
and that for all you know has already rotted
       is mush when they put it in their baskets
and will yield less than they'd hope to earn
       or just enough to face their families
with a sense of pride and guilt with that look you know
       your father will give your mother at home
that promise to find a way to make things work

QUEEN CITY

And why not believe it why not imagine that as Díaz
      surveyed the landscape — even if he didn't —
he saw not just dirt sagebrush not just heat singed on acres
      and acres of desolation but its potential the beauty
he would help instill upon it the pride in naming a piece of land
      after his wife because why see bushes and mirages
and not think of your love And why not believe in this invented
      truth in the way you as a child once believed
that the fort you were building with bricks and branches
      was your own country Estebanland Estebanstonia
that Estebanstan you refused to desert adamant that you
      wouldn't leave the backyard that as night
descended and the owls surveyed the mess you made
      you would sleep in your new home love
what nothing in this world but you could have named

SPI

Father's Day And though we're at the beach
        he's not sitting sleeping not bearing the sun
and forgetting how at work each day it sears
        his face adds a layer of darkness he no longer
tries to understand No today minus the trunks
        my father's dressed like he's about to mow
the lawn but instead of a trimmer he wields
        like a soldier a metal detector ready to scan
the sand find mines I think until he says either
        to himself or me *Treasure* not a word
I thought he knew in English but one that fits his mood
        and prompts him to begin his search
to wander the shore stop and dig through the mounds
        of algae and shells pull out pieces of plastic
or something broken or torn: a rope a necklace a fish
        with tatters of meat and scales still on it
but rotted enough for my father to see it for a moment
        as a creature not yet discovered And as he
tosses it moves on and ambles farther off I believe that after
        decades in this country and of only affording
vacations to the beach he deserves to do what he wants
        to find treasure good enough to unearth keep

RECUERDO: MEXICO, 1997

When our turn comes   we feed quarters
down the slot   swing through the turnstile's

rusted arms   I look up   shield my face from
a sun that still feels American   And as the city

shudders in and out of focus   and the smell
of gravel   grilled meat and onion singes my nostrils

I spot a vendor on the street corner   hawking
in a voice that doesn't match his limp   a pair

of wooden crosses   each of which he thrusts
higher   as though their height will make them

more symbolic   attractive   My mother pulls me
harder   pinches my wrist till it swells into a small

stigmata   and despite what her body language
tells me I shouldn't see   the shop owners shouting

their latest discounts   the soldiers surveying
the pothole-riddled sidewalks and streets

I gaze at a row of old seated women begging
with barely any teeth   mouthing phrases

of a practiced speech   exposing   without shame
the same decay that's brought my mother back

to her home country   and that aggravates
her enough to ignore them   to let our bodies

toss our shadows like change at their feet

RECUERDO: SOMNAMBULIST

Full moon   And again your father
in briefs and with one sandal   stands

at the edge of the yard   cursing God
the stars   cursing the chained dogs

that begin to howl   One by one   the lights
come on   and because he thinks they're souls

disguised as orbs   he damns them all
curses more and more   until he's had

enough   and with the logic locked
in his sleeping mind   starts collecting

whatever's near   water hose   bags
toy trucks he tosses   along with everything

else   into the barbecue pit   laughing
as he drops them in   and believing

that when he ignites his invisible match
flicks it in the grill   the answers he wants

will be revealed

RECUERDO: WARDROBES

Because treasure is found in darkness
I open my parents' closet   inhale the scent

of unmarked boxes   broken high heels
plastic coverings over my mother's short

and slender-fitted dresses   each hanging
like a carcass of fabric I reach out and touch

fanning my fingers against the crinkled cotton
the hems sewn with labyrinths of neon-colored

gardens   the waistlines too thin to bear
the weight of her second life   those unintended

measurements of a mother   wife   One child
one attempt at a shotgun marriage later

and age has clichéd her skin with cellulite
and wrinkles   with a silence arthritically angled

across her back   as her daily posture hunches
further into its obligations   and a sense

that even if she completes them   sweats
and blots her blouses with a résumé of stains

her body   like all bodies not immunized
to the circumstances they've inherited

can't reverse what she's already gained
or regain the way her younger legs swept

across the living room's torn linoleum
where my father   not yet the man I'd equate

with a worn-out wardrobe of Levi's and hardhats
would take her by the hips and hands

and lead her back and forth and back
becoming nothing more than a fluorescent blur

than scenes I'm not sure were ever real
but which I recreate as I unhook the wooden

hangers   pull her dresses down   and twirl
my mother's image around before it slips

from its threadbare form

RECUERDO: LA MIGRA

Then *la migra* came
and what was at first a traffic stop

at a Wendy's parking lot became
a blur of lights   patrol men   police

And inside the back of a pickup
in that camper that gave the truck

the feeling of animal control
sat an old man   cuffed   disheveled

in as much shock as his face
rendered him in the window   but aware

of what came next when the agents
began their paperwork   when the hour

bled into small talk   laughter
into long suspicious surveys of the lot

as though a person of interest were near
or as though they knew the status

of the men inside the restaurant
and were waiting for one to come out

for any of those fathers who sat
watching   as my father watched

to drop their drinks and fries
and in the way they gave their wet skin

to a new land   surrender freely
to the cold custody of night

WILDCATS

They grow beautiful in October rush the field
       train their minds bodies And when scrimmages
are over and the stadium fills up we watch them gallop
       like an ancient army like a team of boys
who believe themselves men who in shiny helmets
       glossy pads attack attack attack gain yards
and yards of land until they've reached the end and
       with points on the board and a sense they can conquer
the world run back with territory to defend and with every right
       to claim they've been anointed as the chosen ones
as the gods we see them as when they walk the halls
       command the sea of bodies to part and proclaim
to all who chose to listen that when Friday comes around
       and that first play is called they'll sacrifice themselves
won't stop till their job is done

WESMER

Friday so we squeeze into someone's Mustang
        cruise neighborhoods streets till we arrive
at the outskirts of town where at the edge of some
        abandoned plaza's parking lot we find the man
we need the man who last week took our twenty
        if it meant he could buy a forty for himself
And so again we chat ask without really caring
        what's new on the streets respond to what he
says with a *Cool Awesome Badass* with a nod and shoulder
        shrug like we were old friends And like old friends
we again expect a favor say two packs this time say
        whatever's left is for him and though he doesn't
object grunts as a sign of yes we tell him we're going
        to someone's house where we hope to party all night
and where we hope if we don't crash on the couch
        that when we head home there'll be a bed
for us to rest our mistakes

HARLINGEN

Because secrets age into gossip
      my mother tells me that weeks ago
when they got home my cousin went
      to the bathroom and in the tub
scrubbed himself with bleach soap tried
      to clean and wipe off this skin
because the darkness he claimed was ugly
      wrong was so different from
the white people he saw in Harlingen
      My mother laughs says how ridículo
this sounds but she too must have thought
      once before what I'm thinking now
that my skin is lighter than hers that I
      on certain days can pass for white
or at least as someone undefined a shade
      that doesn't assume I speak my mother's
tongue but that paints me as something
      between exotic and other a boy who may
or may not look at himself in the mirror run
      his hand along his neck chest
and wonder as he digs his nails in what flesh
      he can uncover what body
he's long oppressed

BASILICA OF OUR LADY OF SAN JUAN DEL VALLE

At your sendoff you learn of it the crazy pilot
         the plane crash how the church burned all day
became a mound of rubble ash Your uncle midway
         through wings and beer asks what you think
of that if tomorrow when you get on the plane you believe
         you'll land arrive ready for college life
for the sea of chicks the parties where everyone's trashed
         And as he laughs slaps your back you're sure
he's asking if you'll miss this place or miss if not the food
         your family friends the feeling of being with people
who look like you who have your last name accent
         who even if they don't know Spanish speak
as if they do and respond with that silence you give
         your uncle that smile that says both yes and no
and that confesses that once you leave no matter how long
         or brief no part of you can ever return

BROWNSVILLE

In Brownsville you recall the word
     how the boys at school tossed *mojado*
back and forth let it cake like saliva
     on their lips And you remember
how it spilled from your mouth once
     not knowing your father was near
or if he heard though you're sure he did
     that he didn't need to understand
the English you embraced it with to know
     what you meant that you were describing
someone like him perhaps a boy dark enough
     to guess he crossed in the dead of night
the Rio Grande and that once here no matter
     how well he spoke or dressed
he couldn't escape the consequences of his skin
     or at least the name-calling the otherness
you and your light complexion never felt
     and never would even though you
repented vowed to never use the word again
     and remember when you find yourself
in Brownsville or any city for that matter
     your father rising from the river
ready to learn a new kind of silence

ABOUT THE AUTHOR

Esteban Rodríguez is the author of the collections *Dusk & Dust* (Hub City Press, 2019), *Crash Course* (Saddle Road Press, 2019), *In Bloom* (SFASU Press, 2020), and *(Dis)placement* (Skull + Wind Press, 2020). His poetry has appeared in *Boulevard*, *The Rumpus*, *Shenandoah*, *TriQuarterly*, and elsewhere. He is the Interviews Editor for *EcoTheo Review*, an Assistant Poetry Editor for *AGNI*, and a regular reviews contributor for *PANK* and *Heavy Feather Review*. He lives with his family in Austin, Texas.

OTHER SUNDRESS TITLES

What Nothing
Anna Meister
$16

To Everything There Is
Donna Vorreyer
$16

Hood Criatura
féi hernandez
$16

nightsong
Ever Jones
$16

Maps of Injury
Chera Hammons
$16

JAW
Albert Abonado
$16

Lessons in Breathing Underwater
H.K. Hummel
$16

Bury Me in Thunder
syan jay
$16

Dead Man's Float
Ruth Foley
$16

Gender Flytrap
Zoë Estelle Hitzel
$16

Blood Stripes
Aaron Graham
$16

Boom Box
Amorak Huey
$16

Arabilis
Leah Silvieus
$16

Afakasi | Half-Caste
Hali F. Sofala-Jones
$16

Match Cut
Letitia Trent
$16

Marvels
MR Sheffield
$20

Passing Through Humansville
Karen Craigo
$16

Divining Bones
Charlie Bondus
$16

CPSIA information can be obtained
at www.ICGtesting.com
Printed in the USA
JSHW030459100321
12399JS00001B/6

9 781951 979140